CH00688763

WALKS FROM THE
PEN-Y-GWRYD HOTEL

Text, photographs and maps © Geoffrey Pocock 2009

Dedication

To Jane and Brian Pullee whose hospitality made the Pen-y-Gwryd a mountaineer's home-from-home.

Published by L&B Publishing

Printed in England at imprintdigital.net

ISBN 978-0-9562992-1-5

All rights reserved. No part of this publication may be reproduced, stored in a retrieval system or transmitted in any form, or by any means electronic or mechanical by photocopying, recording or otherwise without prior permission in writing from the publisher.

Every effort has been made to ensure the accuracy of this guide but the landscape is always changing so we welcome any feedback readers may have.

Please email your comments to guiding@leisure-and-business.co.uk

WALKS FROM THE PEN-Y-GWRYD HOTEL

Geoffrey Pocock

L&B Publishing

CONTENTS

FOREWORD   5
BACKGROUND INFORMATION   6
ABBREVIATIONS AND SYMBOLS   8
THE SNOWDON RANGE   10
    The Snowdon Horseshoe   12
    Pyg and Miners' Track   14
    South Ridge of Snowdon   16
    The Watkin Path   16
    South Flank of Lliwedd and Gallt y Wenallt   18
THE GLYDERS   24
    Glyder Fach, Glyder Fawr and descent to Pen-y-pass 26
    Esgair Felen   26
    South Ridge of Tryfan and Bristly Ridge   28
    The Gribin Ridge   28
    Traverse of the 3000' Glyders   30
    Capel Curig and the Dyffryn low level walk   32
MOEL SIABOD AND CNICHT   34
    Moel Siabod and Carnedd y Cribau   34
    Moel Siabod from Dolwyddelan   36
    Cnicht via Gelli Iago   38
THE CARNEDDAU   40
    Pen yr Ole Wen, Carnedd Dafydd and Carnedd Llewelyn 40
APPENDIX A - A short glossary of Welsh topographical names   42

FOREWORD

The Pen-y-Gwryd is a very special hotel because it offers its guests what they want with no unnecessary sophistication. No fast food, no canned music and no plastic decor; just good food, good beer and wine, and simple but comfortable rooms. The Hotel resonates with the history of British mountaineering from the early Victorian tourists to the 1953 Everest team and the photographs adorning the walls and collections of memorabilia add to the atmosphere. Its guests, young and old, appreciate the tradition of the Hotel which over the years has rightly established itself as one of the homes of British mountaineering. Sharing a common love of the mountains, they come from all walks of life and the conversation after dinner in the erstwhile Smoke Room is wide and varied.

The Pen-y-Gwryd is also special by virtue of its position. No other hotel in Snowdonia offers access to such a range of walks directly from the front door of the hotel itself. For several years, the Pen-y-Gwryd sold a leaflet of walks that can be made directly from the Hotel without recourse to public transport or a car. This was not written because of any compelling environmental concerns but because for a lot of people the working week is a battle of commuting, parking and being herded with other people. The idea of having a hearty breakfast and strolling out of the Hotel to spend the day on the hills before returning to a hot bath and a beer in the Smoke Room with the minimum of hassle is a great attraction of the Hotel.

Many people found the information in the leaflet useful but those with less knowledge of the surrounding hills and, perhaps, less handy with a map and compass needed something more. Hence this booklet.

BACKGROUND INFORMATION

The Hotel

The earliest recorded building on the site is a farmhouse built by John Roberts in about 1810. The farmhouse became an inn, taken over by Harry Owen in 1847 and when he bought the freehold in 1858 he extended the building. Over the next ninety years the Hotel passed through various hands and was continuously enlarged until, in 1947, it was bought by Chris and Jo Briggs. They ran the Hotel for many years during which time it thrived and become once more the home of mountaineering in Snowdonia. In 1953 the Everest team stayed at the Pen-y-Gwryd to train for the successful ascent.

In later years, Chris and Jo's daughter Jane, with her husband Brian Pullee, took over the running of the hotel. Now their sons Nick and Rupert Pullee are in charge.

How to get there

To reach the Pen-y-Gwryd Hotel by road, follow the A5 to Capel Curig and take the A4086 signposted to Llanberis and Beddgelert. The Hotel is found after 5 miles, on the right immediately before the junction with the A498. By rail, the nearest main station is Bangor with hourly buses from Bangor to Llanberis. From there a taxi costs around £20.

Notes for Walkers

Like any hill area, Snowdonia can at times pose problems and be dangerous. There is no need to over-dramatise this; with care you will probably have no problems. However, many of the walks take you into lonely and exposed places where mobile 'phones get no reception. You need to go prepared.

The weather in Snowdonia can vary from warm sunshine to strong winds, thick mist and driving rain or sleet. All these conditions can occur on the same day even in the middle of summer. The mountain tops may be very cold so take an extra layer of warm clothes as well as waterproofs. Away from the Snowdon massif, most paths have sections that are unmarked. Visitors from mainland Europe should be aware that there are few signposts and no proper paint flashes. The likelihood of mist and the lack of waymarks means that you should carry a map and compass and be able to use them.

Timings

The walking times are calculated using a form of Naismith's rule modified to take account of the steepness of the ascents and descents. The times given are for fit walkers who can quite easily undertake an eight-hour hike. They do not include any allowance for photographic or lunch stops.

Orientation

The directions left and right are in the sense of direction of movement of the walker. For rivers the traditional orographical reference to left and right banks as viewed in the direction of flow is used.

Maps, placenames and language

The walks described in this booklet can all be found on the Ordnance Survey 1:50,000 Landranger sheet 115. Walkers who prefer a 1:25,000 map will find that they need both the Explorer maps 17 and 18 to cover the whole area and, indeed, some of the routes. These are unwieldy double-sided maps and a better option is the Harveys Superwalker maps - Snowdon and the Moelwyns, Glyders and Carneddau.

Placenames and the names of topographical features vary from map to map. For consistency within this booklet, I have mostly used the names from the 1:50,000 OS map with the odd addition of a name from the 1:25,000 OS maps where it is helpful. Welsh speakers and students of the Welsh language do not hold some of the names in high esteem (the OS have their noun genders wrong in some places) and I apologise for using them but for navigational purposes there is no alternative. I have adopted the general policy for English language guidebooks of using the local names where they appear on the map but Anglicising those names and words which are more familiar in English.

A short glossary of Welsh topographical features is given in Appendix A.

Transport

Although the idea is to do all the walks without transport there are some bus services that might be useful if you find yourself taking a shortcut or feeling tired towards the end of one of the longer walks. Unfortunately, the services are not always very convenient. The best is the Snowdon Sherpa which in summer months runs regularly from Nant Peris to Pen-y-pass. A much more limited service runs from Ogwen Cottage to Capel Curig.

ABBREVIATIONS AND SYMBOLS

c.	circa (approximately)
dis.	disused
FB	Footbridge
h	hour(s)
km	kilometre(s)
m	metre(s)
min	minute(s)
OS	Ordnance Survey
Resv.	Reservoir

High ground and peak

River and lake

Refreshments

Isolated building(s)

Woodland/Forestry

Fingerstone

Bus stop

Road

Track

Footpath

Track - not on route

Footpath - not on route or shortcut

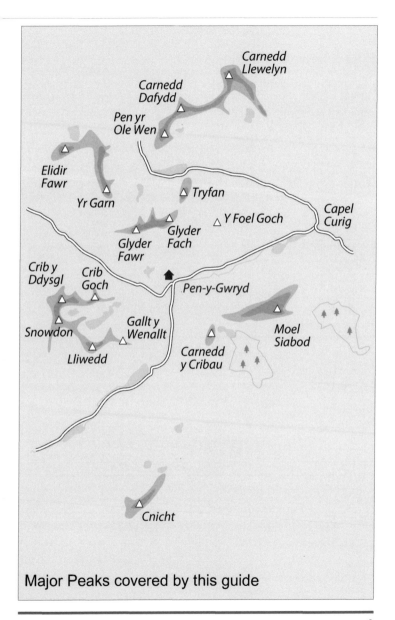

Major Peaks covered by this guide

THE SNOWDON RANGE

Snowdon is the highest peak in Wales and is a popular objective, especially in fine weather when the views from the summit are magnificent. There are several routes starting from the Pen-y-Gwryd. In good conditions the traverse of Crib Goch and Crib y Ddysgl is a superb outing for experienced scramblers who may wish to continue over Lliwedd so completing the Snowdon Horseshoe.

An easier way is to ascend by the Pyg Track and descend by the Miners' Track. A longer but more varied ascent can be made via the south ridge; this is one of the best routes up Snowdon and is rarely busy, even at a Bank Holiday. If a shorter day is needed, a traverse across the southern flanks of Lliwedd to Gallt y Wenallt followed by a steep descent makes a fine outing so long as the visibility is reasonable.

The Snowdon Horseshoe (page 12)

This is one of the most famous ridge scrambles in the UK with exposed scrambling to reach Crib Goch and along the ridge above Cwm Uchaf - to be avoided in strong winds. It is a serious outing in winter conditions. The top part of the Watkin path is somewhat rough as is the last part of the descent from Lliwedd.

The Pyg and Miners' Track (page 14)

This route should present little difficulty to good walkers but in winter conditions it will be icy; above the start of the zig zags crampons may be needed. It is best to ascend by the Pyg Track and return by the Miners' Track since the rough area between the top of the Miners' track and Glaslyn is better in descent.

The South Ridge (page 16)

One of the best routes up Snowdon and much underrated. The approach from the Hotel involves a superb descent of Nantgwynant to the farm buildings at Hafod-y-Llan before briefly joining the Watkin Path on the way to Bwlch Cwm Llan where the South Ridge rises continuously to the summit. To descend, take the Pyg and Miners' Track.

The Watkin Path (page 16)

A splendid route that makes its way up through old mine workings to the bwlch between Snowdon and Lliwedd before turning north-west to join the South Ridge of Snowdon. The final approach to the South Ridge is rough in places.

The South Flank of Lliwedd and Gallt y Wenallt (page 18)

The Horseshoe leaves the ridge after Lliwedd omitting the final "nail" of Gallt y Wenallt. This is a neglected part of the Snowdon range but is nonetheless worth exploring. Navigators will enjoy the pathless section below the summit.

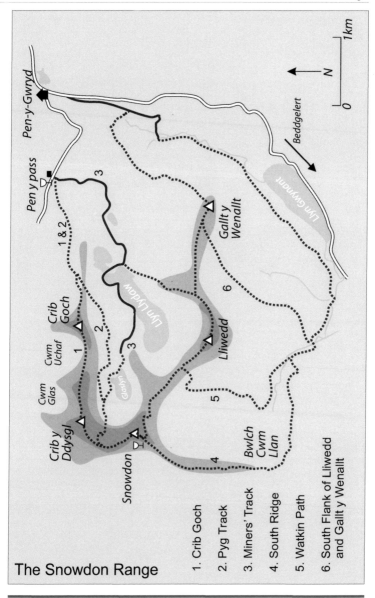

The Snowdon Range

1. Crib Goch
2. Pyg Track
3. Miners' Track
4. South Ridge
5. Watkin Path
6. South Flank of Lliwedd
   and Gallt y Wenallt

The Snowdon Horseshoe

Distance	15km
Ascent	1126m
Time	6h

Walk up the road to the Youth Hostel and car park at Pen-y-pass, **30min**. From the upper car park the Pyg Track is obvious; follow it westwards, gaining height steadily to Bwlch y Moch, **1h15**. The Pyg track carries straight on but for Crib Goch turns up right (sign post) on a good path that leads to the east ridge of Crib Goch.

As you gain height the way becomes less well defined and you will have to make your own way. Work up several little pitches following the scratches and polish on the rock until you reach the final rocky staircase which leads directly to the first, false, summit 2m lower than the true summit which lies on the long ridge that stretches out before you, **2h15**.

Make your way along the ridge. Bold walkers in calm conditions will teeter along the very top; more cautious people will walk just to the left of the ridge using the top as a handrail. After c. 400m you will arrive at the first pinnacle. Skirt this on the left to a small dip then scramble steeply up to continue working over and around more pinnacles keeping close to the apex of the ridge.

At last, easier ground is reached at Bwlch Coch. Ahead lies Crib y Ddysgl which is nicely reached by following the ridge avoiding any temptation to lose height to the right over the cliffs of Clogwyn y Person. From the trig. point on Crib y Ddysgl, **3h15**, an easy descent leads to Bwlch Glas where the Llanberis path is taken to the summit, **3h45**.

If you feel you have had enough go back to Bwlch Glas and go down via the Pyg and Miners' Tracks - see page 14.

To continue on the Horseshoe descend the south ridge for c. 200m distance to reach a finger stone. Turn left down a loose slope until easier ground leads to a junction where the Watkin path descends, **4h15**. Ahead the ground rises to the west peak of Lliwedd which is reached by an amusing scramble over large, stable blocks, **4h45**.

Once on the summit, follow the ridge over the east peak to Lliwedd Bach before descending more steeply to Llyn Llydaw, **5h15**. Do not cross the causeway but turn right on the jeep track to Pen-y-pass and down the road to the Hotel, **6h**.

The final nail in the horseshoe

On the far side of Lliwedd, where the path drops towards Llyn Llydaw, turn right on a broad ridge (only a trace of path) just south of east to Gallt y Wenallt, **5h15**. The descent to the Hotel, described on page 18, is steep and needs care in poor visibility.

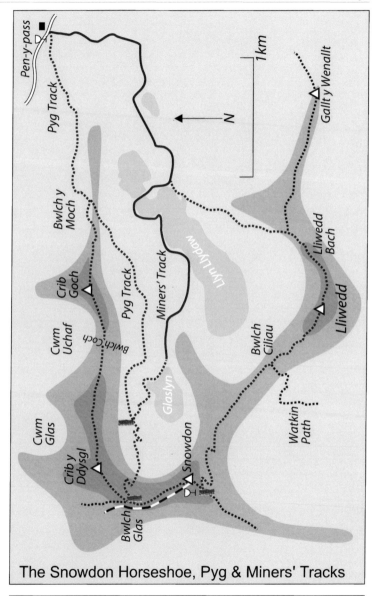

The Snowdon Horseshoe, Pyg & Miners' Tracks

Pyg and Miners' Track

Distance	15km
Ascent	810m
Time	5h

Start as the previous walk to Pen-y-pass and Bwlch y Moch, **1h15**. Ignore the path to Crib Goch which takes off to the right and continue south-west across the southern flank of Crib Goch.

The well-laid path affords magnificent views of the buttresses of Lliwedd on the far side of Llyn Llydaw and, ahead, the towering peak of Snowdon. Above Glaslyn the path turns to the north, then west again where it is joined by the Miners' Track at a finger stone, **1h45**.

The way now becomes a little rougher but still easy to follow as it works its way through old mine workings to the start of the zig zags. These have been considerably improved over recent years to prevent erosion and form a solid staircase to Bwlch Glas, **2h45**. At a further finger stone join the path from Llanberis; turn left and follow it to the summit, **3h**.

When the train is running you will find all and sundry here. Many people, having touched the summit cairn, will turn straight round and start to descend, looking for a quieter place for lunch.

Reverse the route to the fingerstone at Bwlch Glas then turn east down the zig zags to the smaller fingerstone that marks the Miners' Track. Do not be tempted by paths off to the right before this.

Descend to Glaslyn, **3h45**, and a delightful place to stop for lunch.

Below the lake the path gradually turns into a jeep track. Carry on along the shore of Llyn Llydaw and across the causeway, **4h15**, to Pen-y-pass, **4h45**, and down the road to the Hotel, **5h**.

Pyg or Pig?

Early descriptions of this path referred to the Pig Track: Carr, in 1926, noted that "Its name is derived from Bwlch Moch, the Pig's pass.... but .... owing to the fact that the habitués of the Pen-y-Gwryd played a prominent part in the early exploration of this route the form P.y.g Track is sometimes employed."

Carr preferred the more ancient, pastoral word but maps and guides have been ambivalent about it. In the 1950s and 60s the 1:50,000 OS maps used "Pyg" having previously used "Pig", but later 1:25,000 maps maintained "Pig".

Nowadays, most maps use "Pyg" but many writers prefer the alternative. I have stuck with the name on the present OS maps.

Crib Goch rising above Bwlch Moch

Fingerstone where the Miners' track leaves the Pyg Track

South Ridge of Snowdon

Distance	20km
Ascent	1063m
Time	6h15

From the Hotel take the road towards Beddgelert. After c. 300m cross a stile on the right; continue down the old Beddgelert road to the Cwm Dyli power station, **30min**. Go through the main gate then a smaller gate and cross a stone bridge before turning left to cross the pipeline. Initially the path stays fairly close to the river then, crossing a number of stiles, it rises through woodland. At the end of a short, wooden, causeway keep up high ignoring any paths that lead down to the Llyn Gwynant.

Soon the path descends before ascending slightly across an open area to arrive at some old mine workings. Continue on a track, past a building where several small signposts lead the way to the farm buildings at Hafod-y-Llan, **1h45**.

Cross a bridge and immediately turn sharp right across another bridge. Go north-west, not much of a path, aiming for the edge of the copse above. Fairly soon the way becomes clear and a stile appears up on the right; this leads to Gallt y Wenallt, see page 18. Turn away from the stile and descend to the river where a clapper bridge leads across to join the Watkin path, **2h**.

Follow the Watkin path past the waterfalls to a level section where a path goes up left to a dismantled tramway. This is a good path but the turn-off may not be obvious; if you get

to a bridge you have gone too far. At the top of the path turn right onto the old tramway and follow it for c. 250m before striking across the open hillside (traces of a path) to the obvious path leading to Bwlch Cwm Llan, **3h**.

At the Bwlch, turn right to gain the south ridge of Snowdon and climb the fine rocky ridge past the junction with the Rhyd-Ddu path to the summit, **4h15**.

There are various possibilities for descent but the Pyg track then the Miners' track is the shortest, see page 14.

The Watkin Path

Distance	20km
Ascent	1063m
Time	6h15

Follow the route described above to the clapper bridge, **2h**, cross the river and follow the obvious path beside its right bank. Re-cross the river shortly after the path goes off left to the South Ridge. Continue close to the left bank of the river past the Gladstone rock where a plaque records the opening of the path by Gladstone in 1892.

Pass by some derelict quarry buildings, **2h30**, and turn north-east making height steadily to Bwlch Ciliau, **3h30**.

At the Bwlch, the path turns north west and is almost level for some 750m before it steepens and becomes quite loose in places until it joins the South Ridge which is followed to the summit, **4h15**.

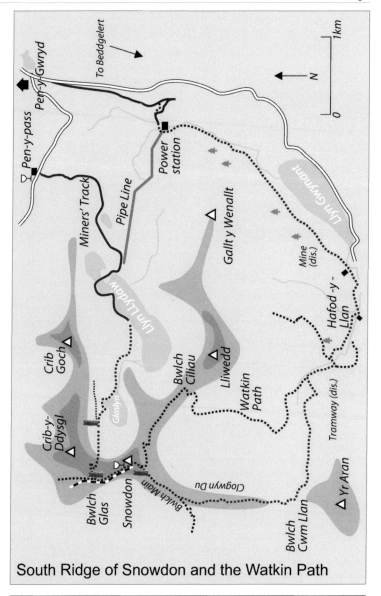

South Ridge of Snowdon and the Watkin Path

South Flank of Lliwedd and Gallt y Wenallt

Distance	15km
Ascent	720m
Time	4h45

The area south of Lliwedd is unfairly neglected and Gallt y Wenallt is seldom visited but it offers delightful walking and a solitude not found amongst the peaks to the north. The route described here is one of many excellent walks in Don Hinson's books.

Although not a long walk, with only a modest amount of ascent, it is quite challenging. The final approach to Gallt y Wenallt has little in the way of a path and the route beyond the pipeline requires careful navigation.

To start, follow the previous route down the old Beddgelert road and past Llyn Gwynant to Hafod-y-Llan, **1h45**, and go up to the stile where the path turns down left towards the clapper bridge and the Watkin path. Turn right and cross the stile to enter the wood.

Follow the path to open hillside and continue across another stile into a narrow defile between grassy banks at the end of which there is a good view of Gallt y Wenallt ahead and Llyn Gwynant below. Go through a gate on the left and ascend half left for a short distance before swinging right on a grassy path. At a wall on the left, by a small bluff go diagonally left and after c. 100m cross a stream to arrive at some ruined buildings, **2h30**. Go past some mine spoil and, with little in the way of a path, head north-east to a shallow depression in the ridge to the

left of Gallt y Wenallt. At the ridge crest turn right to the summit, **3h15**.

The descent starts with a number of steep little noses but soon eases by a ruined wall on the left; continue down the crest to a rough, stony area and another wall. Ahead, there is a ruin by a bluff and a large patch of bracken. Head for the right of the ruin where a bridge over the pipeline can be seen; descend to the pipeline, **3h45**.

Cross the pipeline and ascend a small hill. Below and half right is a solid wall and two ruins which lie on the path. Do not head directly to the wall but drop straight down to the Afon Glaslyn. After heavy rain it may be difficult to cross the river; it gets easier upstream. On the far side follow the river to the wall noted above. Now work down past the ruins and break away to the right under an overhead power cable to the river where a faint path leads back to the old Beddgelert road, **4h15**.

Follow the road to the Hotel, **4h45**.

Don Hinson's Books

I discovered this route in Don Hinson's book - *New Walks in Snowdonia*. This guide and its companions: *Walks in North Snowdonia* and *Walks in the Snowdonia Mountains*, contain a multitude of well-described walks of a variety of lengths.

Highly recommended.

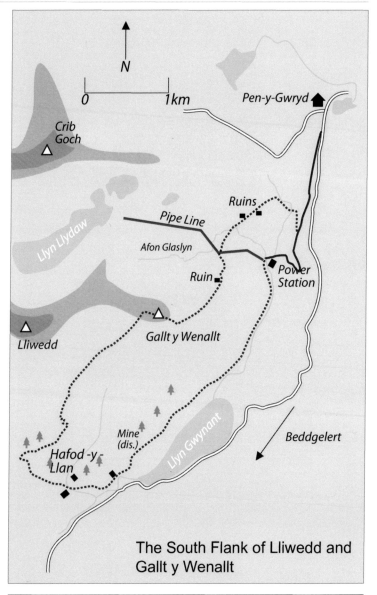

N

0   1km

Pen-y-Gwryd

Crib Goch

Ruins

Pipe Line

Llyn Llydaw

Afon Glaslyn

Ruin

Power Station

Lliwedd

Gallt y Wenallt

Beddgelert

Mine (dis.)

Llyn Gwynant

Hafod -y- Llan

The South Flank of Lliwedd and Gallt y Wenallt

Clapper bridge leading to the Watkin Path from Hafod y Llan

The Crib Goch pinnacles, Crib y Ddysgl and Snowdon

Lliwedd

The stile to cross on the way to the Glyders

Castell y Gwynt with Snowdon in the distance

Llyn y Cwn

View north-east from Elidir Fawr

Dolwyddelan Castle

THE GLYDERS

The Glyders lie to the north of the Hotel and provide a delightful day out. Many variations are possible including a traverse of all of them - from Tryfan to Elidir Fawr - in a day, returning to the Hotel by way of the Llanberis pass.

Glyder Fach and Glyder Fawr (page 26)

An undemanding walk with magnificent views that is easily done in just over 5 hours. Extending it slightly to visit Esgair Felen is well worth it for the views of Crib Goch.

South ridge of Tryfan and Bristly Ridge (page 28)

A wonderful day out with a modest scramble to get to the summit of Tryfan and more difficult scrambling up Bristly Ridge to Glyder Fach.

Glyder Fawr by the Gribin Ridge (page 28)

The Gribin Ridge rises from Llyn Bochlwyd to join the plateau between Glyder Fach and Glyder Fawr. It is reached by a well-marked path from Bwlch Tryfan.

Traverse of the 3000' Glyders (page 30)

A long day but well worth it for strong walkers. Allow at least eight hours. In the summer when the Sherpa buses run a full service the final section from Nant Peris could be done by bus.

Capel Curig and the Dyffryn low level walk (page 32)

The Dyffryn low level walk was the first project of the Esmé Kirby Snowdonia Trust. The guide book (available at the Hotel) is well worth buying for its content and to support the Trust. The walk has two branches, one north of the road and the other close to Nantgwryd. They both take about two hours to reach the Pen-y-Gwryd. Only the northernmost path, which passes by Esmé Kirby's cottage (Dyffryn Mymbyr) is described in this booklet.

The Miners' Track

As well as the Miners' track in the Snowdon range there is also a Miners' Track on the Glyders. Unlike the Snowdon Miners' track, this was not used for the transport of ore but was used by the miners living in Bethesda to reach the Snowdon mines.

It runs from the Pen-y-Gwryd over the Glyders to the A5.

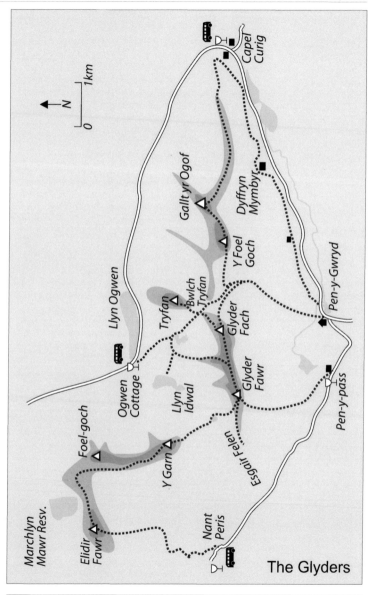

The Glyders

Glyder Fach, Glyder Fawr and descent to Pen-y-pass

Distance	10km
Ascent	813
Descent	4h15

From the Hotel take the Capel Curig road; after 250m cross a stile on the left. Follow the path across a bridge and another stile and head towards a wall and stile. Do not cross this stile but continue making height past yet another stile, c. 15min, until a further stile is reached, **30 min**. See picture on page 21.

Cross the wall and tackle somewhat steeper ground until, after 15min or so, the gradient eases and the path crosses a stream close to a waterfall. Now a break in the ridge above leads to a large marshy plateau and a view of the east face of Tryfan. There are traces of a path amongst the boggy patches to a crossroads 250 m west of Llyn Caseg-fraith, **1h15**.

Turn left up a broad path through broken ground and large blocks to the summit plateau, **2h**. On the right is the top of Bristly Ridge and shortly further on to the left is the Cantilever Stone. Ahead lies the massive pile of boulders of Glyder Fach. Scramble to the top with great care - there are some enormous holes between the blocks; or turn it easily on the right.

To continue to Glyder Fawr keep walking in the same direction towards Castell y Gwynt, the castle of the winds. This is far more easily traversed than Glyder Fach and climbing straight over it is better than the circuitous

path that descends to the left. Both options arrive at a shallow col from where a well-worn path rises to the lip of the Nameless Cwm. Do not be misled by faint descending paths just beyond Castell y Gwynt. From the head of the Nameless Cwm a cairned path leads through a strange landscape of stones and small crags to the summit of Glyder Fawr, **2h30**.

From the summit of Glyder Fawr a vague path marked with some fading red paint spots descends SSW, then south to a flatish area with a couple of small pools. Now turn south-west for a short distance before swinging to the left and arriving at small dip and marshy ground. Ascend a small hillock and gain the ridge above Pen-y-pass which leads through the Hostel garden to the road from where it is only a short walk downhill to the Hotel **4h15**. The direct approach to the Hotel, leaving Llyn Cwmffynnon to the right is extremely boggy and not recommended.

Esgair Felen

From the summit of Glyder Fawr follow a broad ridge west then south west until the ground drops steeply to the Llanberis pass at Craig Nant Peris. The plunging vista below your feet is most impressive but look up and across the pass for the view into Cwm Glas and, above it, the Horseshoe from Crib Goch to Crib y Ddysgl.

To descend, contour east then south-east at a height of c.750m to join the normal path from Glyder Fawr. Allow a good two hours from Glyder Fawr to the Hotel.

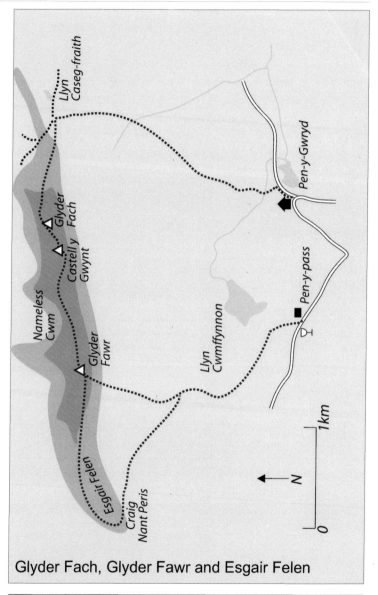

Glyder Fach, Glyder Fawr and Esgair Felen

The Glyders are a scrambler's paradise with grades of difficulty to suit all levels of ability. The routes described here are at the lower end of the grading system: the south ridge of Tryfan is easy for good mountain walkers but Bristly Ridge and the Gribin Ridge require a degree of skill and experience.

Once on the tops you can descend by following the route on page 26 to Pen-y-pass or reverse it down to Llyn Caseg-fraith and take the Miners' Track back to the Hotel; the times below are for the descent via Glyder Fawr and Pen-y-pass.

South Ridge of Tryfan and Bristly Ridge

Distance	13km
Ascent	1048m
Time	5h30

Follow the route described on page 26 to the junction of paths west of Llyn Caseg-fraith, **1h15**. Descend north-west to the head of Cwm Tryfan and traverse across to Bwlch Tryfan, **1h30**.

The way up Tryfan is not well marked, and to a large extent you will have to work it out for yourself. It is probably best to skirt round the south peak to the west where easy blocks and slabs provide a rough but direct passage to the summit, **2h**.

For Bristly Ridge, return to Bwlch Tryfan, **2h15**, and continue south following the course of a stone wall on your left over broken boulders towards the foot of a gully. Go up the gully and at the top move left, across an old wall. Another gully lies ahead; follow it but where it steepens move out to the left then a thin step to the right regains the ridge.

Continue upwards enjoying excellent scrambling. Soon the ridge narrows and a series of pinnacles have to be tackled. Some can be by-passed but it is more fun to surmount them all - making short descents as necessary. All too soon the pleasure is over and the top of the ridge runs out into easy ground and so to Glyder Fach, **3h15**.

The Gribin Ridge

Distance	13km
Ascent	937m
Time	5h

From Bwlch Tryfan follow the excellent path which descends to Llyn Bochlwyd, **1h45**. Cross the outlet stream at its northern extremity and contour round the lake until you reach the junction with a path that leads west to Llyn Idwal.

Turn left, south, and ascend a well-marked path as far as a large grass shoulder, **2h30**. Timid walkers will continue on a path that zig zags up to the west of the ridge. But that misses all the fun and it is much more interesting to tackle the ridge directly. There is excellent scrambling on good rock with fine exposure to the left. Soon, the gradient eases and the route blends into the easy ground between Glyder Fach and Glyder Fawr. Turn right to Glyder Fawr, **3h15**.

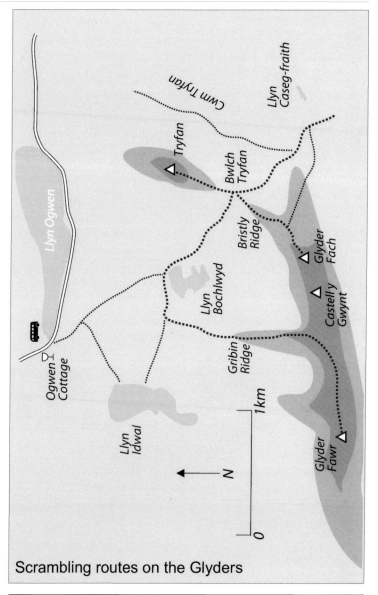

Scrambling routes on the Glyders

Traverse of the 3000′ Glyders

Distance	24km
Ascent	1763m
Time	8h30

This route, along with the southern Carneddau, is much more demanding than any of the other outings described in this booklet. It needs good weather and a strong party that can keep up a steady pace for over eight hours.

Get yourself organised the night before and make an early start from the Hotel immediately after breakfast. Follow the route on page 28 to Tryfan up and down the South Ridge then Glyder Fach via Bristly Ridge, **3h15**. Continue in the same direction over or past Castell y Gwynt to Glyder Fawr, **3h45**.

The descent to Llyn y Cwn is steep and lose, and despite a multitude of cairns is not easy to follow, especially in mist. From the summit keep heading just south of west for c. 60m where a path is cairned down the hillside. There is a second path to the left but this is even less pleasant than the first so take the first offering and follow the line of cairns ignoring those to the left. When in doubt keep right to reach much more pleasant ground by Llyn y Cwn, **4h**.

Y Garn lies straight ahead to the north and after a rough descent it is a great pleasure to stride up an excellent gradient to the summit, **4h45**.

From Y Garn the path loses height, steeply at first, then more easily passing beneath the west flank of Foel-goch and swinging in a gentle arc around the head of the cwm south of Mynydd Perfedd. Now start to make height on grassy paths before a final boulder field leads to Elidir Fawr, **5h45**. Below and to the right of the approach to the summit lies the Marchlyn Mawr reservoir, part of the Llanberis pumped storage scheme for electricity generation.

There is no descent path shown on the map but there is a clear indication on the ground. Follow the clues to a track above Nant Peris which leads directly to the road; the bus stop is just to the left, **6h45**. Opposite is the Vaynol Arms, a good place to wait for the bus; or you can walk back

There are plans to construct a proper path from Nant Peris to Pen-y-pass but at present there is only the road to follow. It takes 90 min to Pen-y-pass where a final downhill stretch leads to the Hotel, **8h30**.

Shortcuts

At Llyn y Cwn, take the path south-west to Nant Peris and walk up the road or take a bus.

From Y Garn descend the east ridge - loose underfoot to start - to Llyn Idwal and Ogwen Cottage; limited summer bus service.

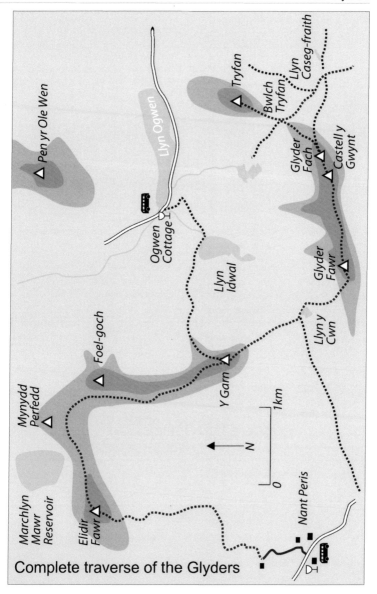

Complete traverse of the Glyders

Capel Curig and the Dyffryn low level walk

Distance	16km
Ascent	715m
Time	4h45

From the Hotel follow the Miners' track (see the description on page 26) as far as Llyn Caseg-fraith, **1h30**. Go east up the broad ridge to the summit of Y Foel Goch, **1h45**, descend north-east to the col then gain 40m to the summit of Gallt yr Ogof, **2h**.

The descent is not well marked but there are no difficulties in finding a way round the rim of Nant y Gors and down to Bwlch Goleuni, using the walls marked on the map for guidance. From here the way to Capel Curig is quite obvious although just before the end there are one or two awkward steps. The path joins a track at Gelli from where it is only a few moments walk to the shops and café, **3h**.

To return to the Hotel, turn right on the track at Gelli and follow it alongside a leat until just before the main road you cross a stile to start the *Low Level Walk*. Initially the route follows a right of way but where it crosses a wall the path goes half right and makes its way up the hillside before contouring above the farm buildings of Dyffryn, **3h45**.

The little lake is man-made and was part of a hydro-electric scheme that supplied Dyffryn for thirty years before the mains arrived. Just beyond the lake go half left and descend to a wall turning half right and continuing in the same direction as the road. Cross several stiles and pass two ruined buildings, **4h15**.

Cross one more wall before descending to the road just east of the Hotel, **4h45**.

Esmé Kirby

Esmé Kirby loved Snowdonia and devoted much of her life to protecting it from unnecessary development. Her early fame was as a central character in her first husband's book - *I Bought a Mountain* - but it was after she retired from sheep farming that she really sprang to fame as a fighter for the preservation of the beauties of Snowdonia.

With her second husband, Peter Kirby, she worked tirelessly to remove eyesores, protect landmarks and maintain (and develop) mountain footpaths.

The path described here was one of the first projects to be approved by the Esmé Kirby Snowdonia Trust in 1995. In the course of the walk, you will pass by Esmé's farmhouse, Dyffryn Mymbyr, where she lived from the 1930s until her death in 1999.

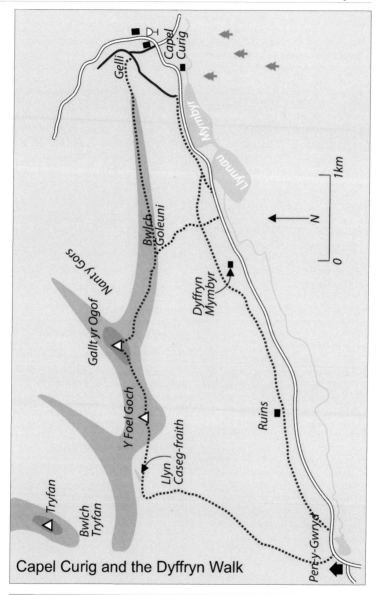

Capel Curig and the Dyffryn Walk

MOEL SIABOD AND CNICHT

To the south-east of the Hotel lies a vast upland area with several peaks and many small lakes. Moel Siabod marks the northern extent of the area which extends south-west to Cnicht. There are no major peaks and few significant paths; consequently, this area receives less attention than other ranges. This is a shame because it has a lot to offer with interesting walks, magnificent views, and a sense of solitude not often found elsewhere.

Moel Siabod and Carnedd y Cribau

Distance	15km
Ascent	853m
Time	4h45

The views from Moel Siabod are exceptional. Looking across to Snowdon one's gaze moves to the left to embrace Lliwedd, Yr Aran and round to Mole Hebog. To the right rise the Glyders and beyond, Carnedd Llewelyn pears out above Gallt yr Ogof. An ascent of Moel Siabod with a direct return to the Hotel makes good use of a half day.

With a little more time it is well worth crossing Carnedd y Cribau to Bwlch y Rhediad before descending into Nant Gwynant and returning to the Hotel by way of the old Beddgelert Road.

The first part of the route is the obvious hill opposite the Hotel and the only difficulty is reaching it across a boggy area. From the top of the first rise, go directly towards an old wall in a south-easterly direction. Work steadily upwards to Bwlch Rhiw'r Ychen which looks down to the twin lakes of Llynau Diwaunydd and the forest above Dolwyddelan, **1h**.

Turning left, follow the obvious route alongside the fence until you cross a

stile and some rocky, open ground to the summit of Moel Siabod **2h**. The return to the Hotel takes just over an hour reversing your ascent.

The longer route down also reverses the ascent but at Bwlch Rhiw'r Y'Chen turn south, alongside a fence, to Carnedd y Cribau, **3h**.

From here the descent crosses complex terrain with a variety of rocky and boggy challenges. The path varies from good to barely visible and often there is a trace of a path on both sides of the fence. A final descent over steepish ground brings you to Bwlch y Rhediad, **3h30**.

Turn west on pleasant ground, cross some old walls and enter a wood before reaching the Beddgelert road at a stile. Immediately opposite another stile crosses a fence and it is only a matter of minutes before the old Beddgelert road is reached at Hafod Rhisgl, **3h45**.

Turn right along the road and track back to the Hotel, **4h45**.

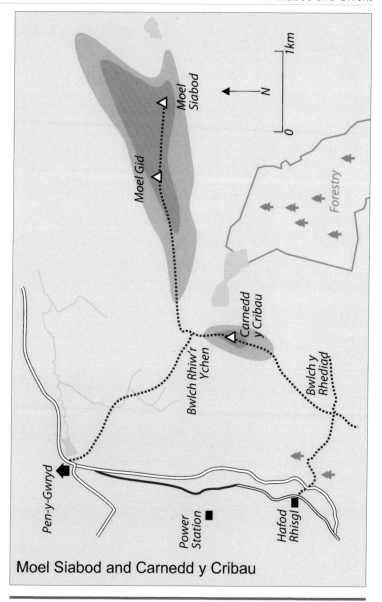

Moel Siabod and Carnedd y Cribau

Moel Siabod from Dolwyddelan

Distance	24km
Ascent	1040m
Time	7h

Climbing Moel Siabod from Dolwyddelan offers a good walk and a fine scramble as well as a visit to Dolwyddelan Castle and a pub lunch - if you can walk after a beer!

From the Hotel go down the old Beddgelert road. Just before the farm buildings at Hafod Rhisgl a gate on the left has a partially obscured sign; pass through the gateway and take a faint path leading up to a stile and the main road, **45min**. If you get to the entrance to Hafod Rhisgl, on the right, you have gone too far. Turn back for a few metres and the sign on the gate should be obvious.

Cross the main road, go over a second stile and follow a path, some signs, through trees then open ground to old walls and sheepfolds and to the boundary fence at Bwlch y Rhediad, **1h30**.

Keep going east, avoiding the boggy patches where possible, to a small copse. Turn right and descend to a river which is crossed to reach a rough track that leads to Coed Mawr, **2h15**. Leave the farm buildings behind you and join a minor road through Blaenau Dolwyddelan as far as Pen-y-rhiw where a track goes off left to Dolwyddelan Castle, **3h**.

Beyond the Castle join the main road and follow it to Dolwyddelan, **3h15**. There is a pub here and in the lane

opposite a general store selling cold drinks.

Take the left turning - *Tan Rallt* - at the crossroads and where the lane turns back left on itself go right on a track for c. 80m then turn half left towards a house. Follow the path to the south of the house to a track which leads into the forestry plantation.

The map is helpful but cannot keep up with all the changes in the forestry tracks so work your way to the north-west corner of the plantation. Here a path ascends through trees then pleasant open ground to Llyn y Foel, **5h**. Keeping south of the lake go west to the east (Daear Ddu) ridge of Moel Siabod which is ascended with some easy scrambling to the summit, **5h45**. Allow 1h15 to descend to the Hotel.

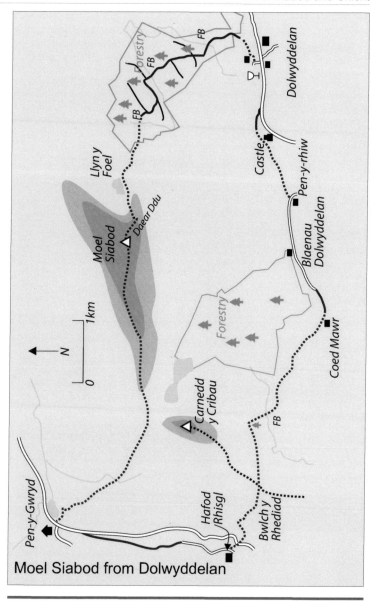

Moel Siabod from Dolwyddelan

Cnicht via Gelli Iago

Distance	23km
Ascent	897m
Time	6h30

Go down the old Beddgelert road past the turning to the power station, across a bridge then a cattle grid where the surface becomes tarmac. Continue on this until it joins the main Beddgelert road by Llyn Gwynant, **45min**.

Walk along the main road for c. 800m to a gate on the left, signposted. Pass through the gateway and go south on a track for a short distance to some dry stone steps that lead off to the left. Take these and follow a path which cuts off the bends in the track before rejoining it. Go left and immediately leave the track and follow a path by a wall. Beyond a wall on the right are a couple of derelict buildings. Don't break the wall attempting a short cut as others have done but carry on until the wall ends and a nice grassy path leads to them, **1h15**.

Go through a gap in the wall to the left of the buildings and turn south into a pine wood. Continue through trees for c. 900m then cross a pleasant open area. On the far side of this cross a bridge over Afon Llynedno and turn left to arrive at a bend on a minor road. Follow this to Gelli Iago, **1h45**.

Just beyond a rough parking place on the left there is a gate but no signpost; pass through the gateway and follow the track past a house where a well-marked path ascends beside a stream to Bwlch y Battel, **2h45**.

Cross the stile and turn half left across a boggy area, over an old wall, swinging gently south-east before making height towards a scree-filled gully. Struggle up this to emerge on a grassy plateau and the junction with the path from Croesor.

On the left a nice ridge rises up to the summit of Cnicht. Just to the right of the bulk of the ridge there is an excellent scramble - do not be tempted by the tame path that bypasses it to the right - to the summit of Cnicht, **3h30**.

To return to the Hotel, descend north-east towards Llyn yr Adar; although no path is shown on the map the way is quite clear on the ground. At the lake turn almost east to gain the crest of the ridge and a solid boundary fence, **4h15**.

Follow the ridge past Llyn Edno - stopping to look back at the views of coast and sea - and continue more or less north to Bwlch y Rhediad, **5h15**. Turn west on pleasant ground, cross some old walls and soon enter a wood before arriving at the Beddgelert road. Immediately opposite a stile crosses the fence and shortly the old Beddgelert road is reached at Hafod Rhisgl, **5h30**. Turn right up the road to the Hotel, **6h30**.

Continuation via Carnedd y Cribau

See the sketch map on page 35. From Bwlch y Rhediad, continue along the ridge to Carnedd y Cribau, **6h**. Descend to Bwlch Rhiw'r Ychen, **6h15**, and the Hotel, **6h45**.

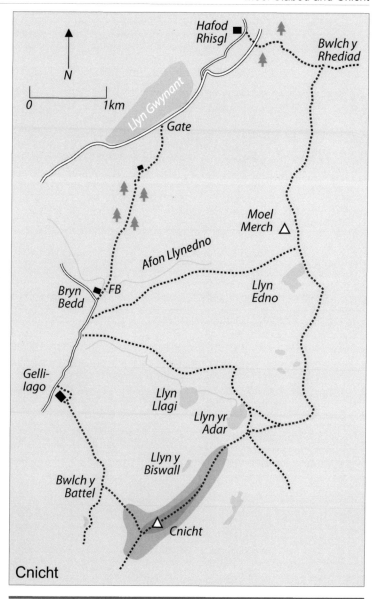

Cnicht

THE CARNEDDAU

The Carneddau are on a large scale; long, undulating ridges and steep drops into huge cwms. At first sight, their distance from the Hotel, 6km to the base of their southern extent and the total height gain, over 1800m there and back, appear to preclude any possibility of a day walk. But it can be done given good weather and a strong party.

Pen yr Ole Wen, Carnedd Dafydd and Carnedd Llewelyn

Distance	24km
Ascent	1813m
Time	8h30

Follow the route on page 26 to just by Llyn Caseg-fraith and descend to the head of Cwm Tryfan where a path strikes off right down the cwm, **1h30**. Follow this as far as the old road by Gwern Gof Uchaf, **2h**. Turn left on the rough track and soon join the A5. Cross the road and take a track past the Midland Association of Mountaineers' hut (MAM) striking off north over a stile before you reach the farm buildings.

Now a steady ascent to Cwm Lloer, boggy in places but well marked by poles that look like nautical cardinal markers. Once into the cwm do not continue towards the lake but swing left to the east ridge of Pen yr Ole Wen where a short scramble leads to a path that winds up through boulders and heather to the summit, **3h45**.

An excellent path leads along the rim of Cwm Lloer past a huge cairn to Carnedd Dafydd, **4h15**. From the summit the path heads east descending slightly to a shallow col from where a good pull up over scree leads to the summit of Carnedd Llewelyn, **5h**.

From the summit descend south-east over slabby ground to a grassy ridge which leads to the rocks above Craig yr Ysfa. A short scramble down brings you to Bwlch Eryl Fargoch. Turn down right on a path, steep at first, to the Ffynnon Llugwy reservoir, **5h45**, where a road goes directly onto the A5, **6h15**.

Cross the road and turn right to the farm at Gwern Gof Isaf. Turn left into the farmyard where a stile leads onto the open hillside. Follow the ridge - Braich y Ddeugwm - by means of intermittent paths and occasional rocky patches to Llyn Caseg-fraith, **7h45**.

Pick up the track going south across the marshy plateau and follow it back to the Hotel, **8h30**.

A shortcut

About 20 min from Carnedd Dafydd, where the path starts to turn north-east, a broad ridge descends south-east towards the reservoir. There is only a faint path but it is all on grass and not difficult. Keep away from steep ground on the left, aiming initially for a rocky outcrop. Further down avoid the steep crags of Craig y Llyn by moving right. Cross the outlet steam to a metalled road, **5h**. Follow the route above to the Hotel, **7h45**.

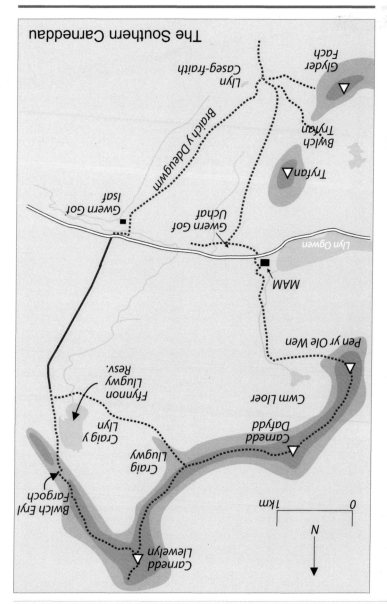

The Southern Carneddau

APPENDIX A - A short glossary of Welsh topographical names

Most of the place-names in Snowdonia are either connected with historical events or describe topographical features. Many of the former are so ancient that with the passage of time they give little indication of their original meaning and are open to significant dispute. The purely topographical names, however, are largely well founded and present fewer problems in translation. The list below covers most of the names used in this booklet.

		Example	
Afon	River		
Aran	High place		
Bedd	Grave	Beddgelert	Gelert's grave
Braich	Arm or branch		
Bryn	Hill		
Bwlch	Pass or saddle		
Carnedd	Cairns		
Caseg	Mare		
Castell	Castle	Castell y Gwynt	Castle of the winds
Clogwyn	Cliff		
Cnicht	Knight		
Coch/Goch	Red	Crib Goch	Red ridge
Crib	Ridge		
Cribau	Comb or crest		
Cwm	Cirque		
Cwn	Dogs	Llyn y Cwn	Lake of the dogs
Dysgl	Dish		
Du	Black		
Dyffryn	Valley		
Esgair	Ridge	Esgair Felen	Yellow ridge
Fach	Small		
Fawr	Large		
Ffynnon	Well or fountain		
Foel/Moel	Bare hill	Foel Goch	Red bare hill
Fraith	Speckled	Llyn Caseg-fraith	Lake of the speckled mare
Gallt	Slope	Gallt y Wenallt	Hill of the white slope
Carn	Eminence		
Celli	Grove or spinney	Celli Iago	James' spinney
Clas	Blue	Glaslyn	Blue lake
Clyder	Block field		

Welsh	English	Example	
Y/Yr	The		
Wen/Wenallt	White	*Pen yr Ole Wen*	Top of the white slope
Uchaf	Upper or higher		
Rhyd	Ford	*Rhyd Ddu*	Black ford
Person	Parson	*Clogwyn y Person*	The parson's cliff
Pen	Peak or top		
Ogof	Cave	*Gallt yr Ogof*	Hill of the cave
Nant	Brook		
Mynydd	Mountain	*Mynydd Perfedd*	Middle mountain
Moch	Pigs	*Bwlch y Moch*	Pass of the pigs
Mawr	Large		
March/Meirch	Horse	*Marchlyn*	Lake of the horse
Llyn	Lake		
Lloer	Moon		
Llan	Church		
Isaf	Lower		
Hafod	Summer dwelling		
Cribin	Rake		
Cors	Swamp		